Steamers of the Clyde — & Westeri

P.S. Pioneer at the West Loch Tarbert Pier before sailing to Islay and Jura c.1925

I am delighted to have been asked to write a foreword for this latest book in the series about vessels which were built and operated on the Clyde.

Clyde built ships have always been noted for quality. Many ships built on the Clyde in recent years continue this tradition of excellence, and some are part of Caledonian MacBrayne's present fleet. These vessels are perpetuating and augmenting the routes established many years ago by the steamers of David MacBrayne and the Caledonian Steam Packet Company, which are described and illustrated in this book.

These more modern vessels provide a greater degree of comfort and convenience than the older steamers, especially on the exposed voyages to the Outer Isles.

Whilst they do not have the nostalgic appeal of the historic steamers they are a logical development from them in meeting the present day needs of the communities in the Highlands and Islands. I am sure that these vessels, their builders and their crews will all live up to the reputation of their predecessors.

Congratulations to John Nicholson, Robin Boyd and Iain Quinn for producing such an interesting as well as accurate record of vessels now gone, which epitomise the work of Scottish shipbuilders, marine engineers and seafarers over the past 185 years, of which we can all be proud.

Colin Paterson C.B.E.
Managing Director (1983-1997)
Caledonian MacBrayne. Ltd.

Steamers of the Clyde & Western Isles

John Nicholson

Although living in Yorkshire, John Nicholson has had a lifelong interest in the Clyde and its steamers ever since his first holiday at Dunoon with his parents in 1930. He found the combination of numerous colourful steamers of the nineteen thirties together with the incomparable scenery of the Firth of Clyde made perfect subjects for his artistic ambitions, as did later visits to Oban and the Western Isles.

He is a member of the Clyde River Steamer Club, the Coastal Cruising Association and the Paddle Steamer Preservation Society. As a 'Waverley' supporter he has designed posters, postcards and other artwork for the steamer since his inaugural poster in 1975.

Robin Boyd was born and still lives in Paisley. Regular childhood holidays on Arran and visits to the Clyde resorts helped to develop a lifelong interest in Clyde steamers. Another early interest in MacBrayne ships has resulted in regular holidays and extensive travelling in the West Highlands. He is a member of both the Clyde River Steamer Club and the West Highland Steamer Club and has been elected to serve as President of each club.

Iain Quinn was born and brought up in Glasgow in a house from which he could view the river Clyde with its panorama of continuous shipping movements. Extended holidays at Dunoon fostered his interest in Clyde steamers of which he has amassed an almost unparalleled collection of photographs and slides. In recent years he has volunteered most of his free time to actively promote the interests of the paddle steamer **"Waverley"**.

Contents

T.S. 'ATALANTA'   J. NICHOLSON.

T.S. Atalanta

The **Atalanta** was built by John Brown & Co. at Clydebank, in 1906, for the Glasgow and South Western Railway and was the first and only turbine steamer in their fleet. Although a screw steamer she was in appearance an almost typical Clyde paddle steamer but without the paddles. Her length was 210 feet, just 10 feet longer than the paddle steamer **Mars** which had been built by the same builders for the company four years earlier. The arrangement of windows on the main deck of the two steamers was also very similar - forward were small rectangular windows whilst aft were larger more square windows. The main difference in the profiles was that on the **Mars** the bridge was abaft the funnel, but forward on the **Atalanta.** Both had a split level mooring deck at the stern.

As is well known the world's first turbine merchant ship, the **King Edward** was built by Denny's at Dumbarton, who built the engines under licence and in collaboration with Parsons on Tyneside (Sir Charles Parsons was the inventor of the steam turbine). The success of **King Edward** quickly led to further orders for the Dumbarton yard, and to Denny's becoming the world's leading shipbuilder for turbine cross-channel steamers and short sea ferries. Other Clyde shipyards realised that the turbine was here to stay, and so had to get their engine builders trained for this new machinery. John Brown & Co. built a set of small turbines for this purpose. They were used as a model for the ones installed later in the Cunarders Carmania and Lusitania. These small turbines were purchased by the G. & S.W.R. Co. who ordered the hull for the **Atalanta** to fit!

The **Atalanta** did not quite achieve her contract speed on trials in May 1906. However she was accepted by the owners, but was returned to the builders for re-boiling at the end of the season, so it would appear that the turbines were not the cause of the speed problem. The **Atalanta** commenced service on the Ayr station, and later in the season served on the Greenock to Ayr route. In 1907 she operated the weekly long day excursion to Stranraer, and in 1908 was on the Arrochar run. In later years she assisted on the Ardrossan - Arran service.

The **Atalanta** served in both world wars. She was requisitioned for trooping in 1915; in December that year she was renamed **Atalanta II** and transferred to minesweeping duties out of Harwich and fitted with two 6 pounder guns. Her partner was the Liverpool & North Wales paddle steamer **St. Seiriol** built by A. & J. Inglis at Pointhouse in 1914. The **Atalanta** was released from war service in April 1919, and after reconditioning assisted the **Glen Sannox** on the Arran service.

In 1923, on the grouping of the various railway companies into just four, the G.W.R., L.M.S., L.N.E.R. and Southern Railway, The G. & S.W.R. and Caledonian Railway became part of the L.M.S., and their locomotives and steamers had to adopt the livery of the parent company. Thus the funnels became buff with black top and a pale red band between the buff and black. However in 1925 the L.M.S. fleets all had the red bands removed and adopted the buff with black top which remained standard until railway nationalisation in 1949. Hulls were black from 1924.

As an L.M.S. steamer her main duty in summer became the secondary Arran service, and the main Arran service in winter, berthing overnight at Ardrossan, but doing an early run from Arran on Monday mornings for Glasgow businessmen who spent the weekends on Arran.

In 1930 she was re-boilered at Dumbarton, and in 1932 was transferred to the Wemyss Bay - Millport station. The 1930 re-boilering would seem to have been hardly justified as only six years later she was sold to the Blackpool Steam Navigation Company, who employed her on excursions from Blackpool and Fleetwood to Barrow-in-Furness (for the Lake District) and later to Morecambe and Llandudno.

In 1940 she was again taken over by the Navy, serving as a net-laying and boom inspection vessel throughout the war, being based at various times at Falmouth, Plymouth, Portsmouth, Southampton and Greenock. She was released by the Admiralty at Methil in November 1945, and was broken up at Ghent in 1946 after a useful and varied life of 40 years.

J.N.

P.S. 'IONA   J. NICHOLSON.

P.S. Iona (III)

The **Iona**, launched in May 1864, was the third vessel of the name to join the fleet of D. Hutcheson & Company. The first **Iona** was built in 1855 by J. & G. Thomson at their Govan yard and was a flush-decked two funnelled paddle steamer for the company's principal service from Glasgow to Ardrishaig. This later became world famous as the Royal Route, following the voyage of Queen Victoria and Prince Albert en route to Balmoral. This first **Iona** was sold to agents of the Confederacy for blockade running in the American Civil War. However, she got no further than Gourock before being run down and sunk by another vessel, probably due to the **Iona** sailing without lights. The second **Iona,** built by the same builders in 1863, sailed for only one season before being sold, again for blockade running, and suffered the same misfortune as her predecessor, this time off Lundy Island. Clyde shipowners were not the only ones to benefit from the high prices being paid by the Confederates for fast vessels, the Isle of Man steamer **Douglas,** built and engined by Robert Napier in Glasgow in 1858 also went to the Confederates. Incidentally it is generally believed that Robert Napier was responsible for the adoption of the famous funnel colours of red with black top and black rings, by three of the earliest steamship companies - The Isle of Man Steam Packet Co. in 1830, The Cunard Line in 1840, and David Hutcheson & Co. (later David MacBrayne Ltd), because Napier supplied the funnels with his engines and those were the colours he used.

The third **Iona** was similar to the one she replaced but slightly larger, and her deck saloons and furnishings were those which had been removed from her predecessor when she was sold. There were alleyways round the saloons, unlike the later **Columba.** In common with other steamers of the period, she carried 3 classes - first, second and steerage. First class passengers enjoyed every luxury available at that time including, in the after part of the vessel, a superb 60ft. long saloon decorated in white and gold, ladies and gentlemen's retiring rooms, etc.

The second class saloon was forward on the same deck, less luxuriously furnished but still of a high standard, whilst steerage was further forward on the lower deck.

The **Iona**'s machinery comprised simple oscillating engines and horizontal boilers, the latter replaced in 1875, and again in 1891, this time with a pair of haystacks, which were lighter and reduced the ship's draught; they also had a much longer life, lasting 45 years. At the same time the funnels were moved closer together and lengthened, greatly improving the steamer's appearance. Other improvements were the provision of steam steering gear and Chadburn's engine room telegraphs, and replacement of the wooden paddle floats with steel ones. In this later condition the **Iona**'s profile was most impressive with her great length and well-proportioned funnels. The finishing touch was the treble gold lining round the hull, not yellow paint as in the later vessels of more austere times!

The **Iona** commenced service in June 1864 from Glasgow calling at Greenock, Kirn, Dunoon, Innellan, Colintraive, Tighnabruaich and Tarbert to Ardrishaig, from whence many of her passengers would continue their journey by steamer through the Crinan Canal, thence by another steamer to Oban, Fort William and Inverness. Around 1903 **Iona** operated an express service from Ardrishaig to Wemyss Bay and return with a late evening sailing.

In the 1914 - 1918 war the **Iona** maintained the Ardrishaig service, but from Wemyss Bay. From 1922 - 1927 she did a summer sailing from Glasgow to Lochgoilhead, and in 1928 was based at Oban for a daily service to Fort William, but replacing the **Columba** on the Ardrishaig service in spring and autumn when traffic did not justify use of the larger steamer. In March 1936 she was sold, along with the **Columba,** to Arnott, Young & Co. and broken up at Dalmuir, after a remarkably long and successful career of 72 years.

J.N.

P.S. Glen Sannox

The **Glen Sannox** was launched from the yard of J. & G. Thomson at Clydebank on 26 March 1892, went on trials on 1 June and achieved a speed of over 20 knots - a record for any Clyde paddle steamer. The following week she commenced service on the route for which she had been specifically designed from Ardrossan to Brodick, Lamlash, Kingscross and Whiting Bay. On weekdays she combined this with cruises from these piers to Campbeltown Loch, Round Arran or Round Ailsa Craig.

The **Glen Sannox** became an immediate favourite with the people of Arran, ousting the hitherto popular Caledonian **Duchess of Hamilton.** She was more than a match for the 'Hamilton' in speed and in her luxurious accommodation. On many occasions the 'Hamilton' left Ardrossan before the 'Sannox', yet the 'Sannox' easily passed her to arrive at Brodick first. The **Duchess of Rothesay** was the only steamer reputed to have beaten her on one occasion. Another time, on a cruise round Bute in 1893 the **Glen Sannox** did the cruise from Rothesay back to Rothesay, with a call at Tighnabruaich, in just under two hours! This compares with 2 hours or more taken by the **Jeanie Deans** in the 1950's! In 1920 she had a neck and neck race with the crack turbine **Queen Alexandra** between Innellan and Rothesay, in which the turbine eventually had to acknowledge defeat, and this when the paddler was 29 years old!

Views differ as to whether the **Glen Sannox** was the best looking of all Clyde steamers. Certainly she was both graceful and impressive, giving a sense of power with her tall red funnels and G. & S.W.R. livery of French grey hull, white saloons, teak beading round the hull, and gold lining and lettering on the white paddle-box.

She made a pleasing sight from almost any angle, possibly best of all from a stern view showing her superb counter stern. In some other views I feel that the after deck appears too short in comparison with the very long foredeck, but that is just a personal opinion.

Internally the **Glen Sannox** had large light and airy saloons tastefully decorated and furnished. The after saloon was particularly spacious with large curtained windows, not only on either side but all round the after end. It was lavishly carpeted with a floral pattern, and plain contrasting runners along the whole length of the room. Even the white ceiling was decorated with a neat floral pattern.

In the first world war the **Glen Sannox** was requisitioned early in 1915 for trooping, but made only one round trip to France before being sent back to the Clyde as being unsuitable for the English Channel. With so many other steamers away she proved invaluable in maintaining the Arran lifeline albeit at reduced speed to save coal. The war over, she had a busy season in 1919; in 1921 and 1922 she gave Round Arran cruises in addition to her regular ferry runs, and still maintained an average speed of 18 knots. In 1923 she became an L.M.S. steamer, retaining her grey hull but with her funnels spoiled by the tricolour buff, red and black. After overhaul in 1924 she reappeared with the now universal L.M.S. livery of black hull and buff black-topped funnels. In September 1924 the **Atalanta** took over from the **Glen Sannox**, until she was permanently replaced by the second **Glen Sannox** in 1925. This steamer, the triple screw turbine built by Wm Denny & Bros. at Dumbarton, was similar to the **Duchess of Argyll** built by them in 1906, but with machinery improvements, particularly greater astern power. She too became popular with the people of Arran. This vessel was in turn superseded by a third **Glen Sannox** in 1957, a motor vessel built by the Ailsa shipyard at Troon and designed for the carriage of motor vehicles and passengers. The paddler was broken up at Port Glasgow in 1925.

J.N.

P.S. Jupiter

The **Jupiter** was a superb paddle steamer with a length of 230ft., beam 28ft, depth 9ft. and a gross tonnage of 394. She was built by J. & G. Thomson at Clydebank, launched in March 1896 and ran trials in May when she exceeded the expectations of the builders and owners - the Glasgow & South Western Railway Company. She averaged 18.5 knots on two runs over the Skelmorlie measured mile. The **Jupiter** was similar to, but slightly larger than the Caledonian Company's **Duchess of Rothesay** which had been built at the same yard the previous year. Unlike the **'Rothesay'** her navigating bridge was abaft the funnel; this continued to be standard practice for G. & S.W.R. vessels with the **Juno** of 1898 and **Mars** of 1902, while the Caledonian Company's **Duchess of Hamilton** of 1890 and all their subsequent steamers had the bridge forward of the funnel. North British steamers continued to have the bridge abaft the funnel until after the 1914 - 1918 war.

Unlike the **Duchess of Rothesay**, the **Jupiter**'s main deck was plated right up to the bow, which gave a neater appearance and must have reduced wind resistance by providing a fine streamlined entrance instead of the flat front of the forward saloon of the Caledonian steamer. The **Jupiter** started life in the attractive colours of the G. & S.W.R. Company, which she retained until the grouping of the railway companies in 1923, when she adopted the first L.M.S. funnel colour of buff with a broad red band and black top, but retaining the grey hull. The following year the hull became black, and later that year the red band on the funnel was made much narrower. In 1925 and for the rest of her life the funnel became buff with black top.

The **Jupiter**'s machinery was a compound diagonal engine, taking steam from a double-ended navy type boiler with a forced draught furnace giving greater efficiency and consequent saving in fuel. She was also more powerful than her predecessors and sturdily built for all year round work. She was based at Greenock, and until the 1914 - 1918 war sailed from Princes Pier to Arran via the Kyles of Bute, with a midday sailing from Brodick to Ardrossan and back. During the 1914 - 1918 war she was employed on minesweeping in the Dover area with the name of **Jupiter II**.

She was reconditioned in 1920, after which she was based at Greenock. From Princes Pier she ran a varied programme of excursions: Mondays and Wednesdays Round the Lochs calling at piers to Millport, then round Garroch Head and through the Kyles to Dunoon, Loch Long and Loch Goil. This cruise was generally conceded to be the most popular excursion on the Clyde. It embraced in one day a wide range and variety of scenery which could only be equalled by spending several days on board the various Excursion Steamers. Tuesdays and Thursdays she sailed to Ayr and on Saturdays did an afternoon cruise to the Kyles. On some Sunday afternoons she did a cruise round Bute. In the early 1930's the Ayr sailings were changed to Mondays and Fridays with a programme of shorter afternoon sailings midweek which presumably were more profitable than long day cruises by making calls at more pick up points.

After 1934 she was relegated to the service runs from Wemyss Bay to Millport with calls at Largs. At the end of 1935 the **Jupiter** was withdrawn from service and sold to T. W. Ward Ltd. of Sheffield and broken up at Barrow-in-Furness.

She can be regarded as a most successful, useful and popular steamer with a life of 39 years. After a lapse of one year the name **Jupiter** was given to a new paddle steamer built at the Fairfield yard in 1937 along with an almost identical sister ship **Juno**. These two sisters, carrying on the old G. & S.W.R. names, were also extremely good looking vessels, like their earlier namesakes, despite having their paddle-boxes concealed following the fashion set by **Mercury** and **Caledonia** in 1934. They had two well spaced funnels, two masts and teak wheelhouse and bridge. They were useful 'dual purpose' ships, providing comfortable lounges and observation saloons appreciated by passengers, as well as being excellent goods carriers with ample clear deck space amidships. This was important on ferry services in the days before vehicle ferries. Sadly the new **Juno** was sunk by bombing in 1941, but the **Jupiter** served until 1957.

J.N.

P.S. Kylemore

A new paddle steamer was ordered by Captain John Williamson from the yard of Russell & Co. at Port Glasgow in 1897 and was launched on 28 April that year and given the name **Kylemore**. However, before completion she was purchased by the Hastings, St. Leonards-on-Sea and Eastbourne Steamboat Co. Ltd. and renamed **Britannia**. She was the sister ship of the **Strathmore**, also built for John Williamson in 1897 for his Glasgow to Rothesay and Kyles of Bute service. The **Britannia** sailed on the South Coast for about seven years, then returned to the Clyde, having been sold to the Glasgow & South Western Railway Company in 1904 and renamed **Vulcan**. After only 3 or 4 years she was sold again - back to her original owner Captain Williamson, who restored the original name, and she remained 'Kylemore' for the rest of her life. She replaced her sister **Strathmore** on the Glasgow - Rothesay service, on which her consort was the **Benmore**, built at Rutherglen in 1876.

In the 1914 -1918 war she was requisitioned for minesweeping in the English Channel, based first at Dover and later at Harwich. In 1920 she returned to the Clyde, with her bridge now positioned forward of the funnel, and took up the 1.30pm sailing from Glasgow to Rothesay, lying overnight at Rothesay and leaving for Glasgow at 8.15 next morning. This allowed her to do evening cruises from Rothesay, and provided a day trip to Glasgow for holiday makers, bearing in mind that the River Clyde was at that time full of interest with numerous shipyards busy building new ships, both passenger and cargo, to replace losses in 4 years of war. **Kylemore** made this route her own until the White Funnel Fleet came under the control of the L.M.S. in 1935. Although registered in the ownership of Williamson - Buchanan Steamers (1936) Ltd., along with the other White Funnel steamers, **Kylemore** became part of the Gourock fleet whilst retaining the white funnel and flying the blue 'star and crescent' flag. The only noticeable change was that the ventilators were now painted silver instead of brown graining, with insides of the cowls blue instead of red. After a short spell on the Wemyss Bay - Millport and Rothesay service the steamer returned to her old up-river route, on which she continued, until the outbreak of war in 1939.

The **Kylemore** was one of three white funnel paddle steamers which had been absorbed into the L.M.S. fleet in 1935, the others being **Eagle III** built in 1910 and **Queen-Empress** built in 1912. **Kylemore** was the smallest of the trio, with a length of 200ft, breadth 24ft., depth 7.7ft. and gross tonnage 319. Her machinery was compound as was that of **Queen-Empress**, whilst **Eagle III** had a single diagonal engine - the last of that type to be installed in a Clyde steamer. In appearance the **Kylemore** and **Queen-Empress** were very similar, but in my opinion the **Queen-Empress** was the better looking of the two, probably due to having windows rather than portholes in the forward saloon. **Kylemore** retained her white funnel until the war, but **Queen-Empress** appeared with the L.M.S. buff colour in 1938.

Soon after the outbreak of war in 1939 all three were called up by the Admiralty for a second spell of war service, and were quickly converted in local shipyards for minesweeping duties. In May 1940 they all took part in the Dunkirk evacuation; **Kylemore** made three return trips, **Queen-Empress** also made several successful trips, and **Eagle III** was deliberately beached to allow troops to climb aboard and cross her deck to board small vessels which carried them to larger ships in deeper water. She was refloated at dusk and returned to Margate with a full load of troops, and then made two more trips.

Queen-Empress and **Eagle III** survived the war, but were unfit for further service and were sold and broken up at Port Glasgow in 1946. **Kylemore** was bombed and sunk in the Wash in September 1940, having given 43 years of service, including naval service in two wars and her early years on the South coast. Whilst not the last representative of the White Funnel fleet she was the last steamer to sail on the Clyde with the famous white funnel.

J.N.

P.S. "ISLE OF ARRAN"   J. NICHOLSON.

P.S. Isle of Arran

The **Isle of Arran** was one of the relatively few Clyde steamers to have been built up-river from Glasgow, at the shipyard of T. B. Seath & Co. at Rutherglen. One of the others was the **Lucy Ashton** built there in 1888. Mr Seath had transferred his shipbuilding business from Meadowside to Rutherglen in 1856, where the company specialized in building small craft, due to the shallowness of the river. Much of their work consisted of expensively fitted-out steam yachts commissioned by clients who could afford, and received, only the best. Workmanship on all Seath's vessels was second to none. One product of the yard was the screw steamer **Raven** built in 1889 which is still sailing on Lake Ullswater after 106 years, though her steam engine, which was in excellent condition, has now been replaced by a petrol engine for operational economy.

The **Isle of Arran** was launched on 14th May 1892 for Captain Buchanan's Glasgow - Arran service. Her dimensions were: length 210ft. breadth 24ft. depth 7.4ft. and gross tonnage 313. The machinery was constructed by W. M. King & Co. and was a single diagonal surface condensing engine taking steam from a haystack boiler at 60lbs pressure, giving the steamer a speed of 15 knots. The **Isle of Arran** was a roomy and comfortable vessel certified for 1,333 passengers, and was a great favourite with the travelling public. She had a large saloon on the main deck aft, lit by handsome oil lamps, and 'No Smoking' in the saloon was strictly enforced - not a common practice in those days. There was a small tea room, and on the deck below a dining room, and bars for saloon and steerage passengers. An attractive external feature was the burnished copper steam pipe on the front of the funnel.

The **Isle of Arran** was employed on the Glasgow - Arran run until 1898, when the Buchanan brothers gave up this service and transferred her to the Glasgow - Dunoon - Rothesay route, with afternoon cruises to the head of Loch Striven, round Cumbrae, or to the Kyles of Bute. She was not called up for war service until 1917, when she was put on minesweeping duties, at first on the Clyde, but later based at Portsmouth. At the end of the war she also had a spell of transporting troops from Le Havre and Rouen to Paris. During reconditioning, after war service, in 1920 her bridge was repositioned forward of the funnel and a small upper deck was provided above the after companionway and Purser's office - not appreciated by the Purser, with children running around on the deck above, while he was busy with his 'Daily Return'. The **Isle of Arran** had no steering engine, so steering by the 5ft. diameter hand wheel was no easy task, especially in a strong wind. The steamer was now part of the Williamson-Buchanan fleet, with funnel painted white with black top in place of the original black with white band shown in the illustration.

In 1933 the **Isle of Arran** was sold to the General Steam Navigation Company who had been operating steamers on the Thames since 1824, latterly under the name of 'Eagle Steamers'. Their services were from Tower Pier, London to the Kent and Essex resorts, as well as cross-channel excursions from Tilbury with big paddle steamers. However, shortly after the acquisition of the **Isle of Arran** the company ordered a large twin-screw diesel vessel of over 1,000 gross tons from Denny Bros at Dumbarton for the cross-channel excursions from Gravesend and Tilbury. This ship, named **Queen of the Channel,** was a great success, resulting in a similar but even larger vessel, the **Royal Sovereign,** being ordered from Denny's for delivery in 1937. This again was a highly popular and successful ship, and led to Denny's receiving further orders for similar diesel vessels, including the 2,000 ton, 21 knot **Royal Daffodil** in 1939. However, the success and operating economy of the motor ship rendered the **Isle of Arran** redundant after only four years with the company, so she was sold for scrap to T. W. Ward & Co. and she was broken up at Grays, Essex in 1936, after a total service of 45 years, 38 of which were on the Clyde.

J.N.

P.S. Mercury

In 1891 the Glasgow & South Western Railway Company decided to go into the business of operating steamers in conjunction with their rail services to the coast. The Caledonian Railway and the North British Railway were already doing this, and it obviously made sense to control the whole operation rather than rely on independent steamboat owners for the rail connections. So in 1891 they purchased two steamers, the **Scotia** which was running the service from Ardrossan to Arran, and the **Chancellor**, on the route from Greenock to Arrochar. Shortly after this they acquired the 'Turkish' fleet from Captain Alexander Williamson. The G. & S.W.R. was not content for long to be the owner of a fleet of second-hand vessels, so they promptly ordered three new steamers, all to be delivered in 1892. The first of these was the **Neptune**, built by Napier, Shanks & Bell, which was launched on 10 March 1892 and commissioned the following month. The second was the **Glen Sannox.**

The third steamer was the **Mercury**, an identical sister ship of the **Neptune** and built at the same yard. She entered service towards the end of May, and both were employed on the Dunoon, Rothesay and Kyles of Bute service from Princes Pier, though **Mercury** also assisted the **Chancellor** on sailings from Greenock to Arrochar. Dimensions of both steamers were:- length 220.5ft., breadth 26ft., depth 9.2ft. and gross tonnage 378. **Neptune**'s speed on trials was 18 knots, **Mercury**'s even faster at 18.45 knots, making them the fastest steamers of their size on the Clyde at that time. Machinery was twin-crank compound diagonal engines with Navy type boilers. Like the **Glen Sannox**, accommodation and furnishings were of a high standard and their popularity with the travelling public was immediately assured.

Besides these three new steamers, the company was also spending a considerable sum on building a new station at the Princes Pier terminal, which was completed in May 1894. And what a magnificent structure it was, with six impressive red brick towers, and luxurious cover for passengers to walk straight down from train to steamer. Princes Pier was my introduction to the Clyde, and **Mercury** was the first Clyde steamer I sailed on, with my parents, in 1930. We had travelled from Yorkshire by train, over the now famous Settle - Carlisle line, which at that time was the Midland main line from London St. Pancras to Glasgow St. Enoch, on which the crack train was the Thames-Clyde express. When we arrived at St. Enoch we just had to cross the platform to the waiting train for Princes Pier, where the weather on our arrival was grey and misty. However this did not deter my excitement at boarding the steamer for Dunoon, then seeing the ropes being let go, hearing the telegraph ring, and watching the foam as the paddles went first astern, then full ahead. The voyage was all too short and soon Castle Hill and the Church at Dunoon appeared out of the mist and **Mercury** was alongside the pier. My first Clyde steamer trip was over, but this was only the start of the best holiday we had ever had, sailing every day, often on several different steamers. The cost for an 8-day season ticket was £1 each for my parents, and half that for my brother and myself, including evening cruises! Thus began my lifelong interest in the Clyde and its steamers.

Mercury and **Neptune** both served as minesweepers in the 1914 - 1918 war; **Neptune** - named **Nepaulin** when on Admiralty service, was sunk by a mine in April 1917. **Mercury** happily survived, despite having her stern blown off by a mine, and after being repaired lost her bow when she struck another mine. She was repaired again and rejoined the G. & S.W.R. Company in 1920 and in 1923 became part of the L.M.S. fleet, where she served on various services until the end of 1933, when she was withdrawn and sold to T. W. Ward Ltd and broken up at Barrow. She was replaced in 1934 by a new **Mercury**, also a paddle steamer but with 'concealed' paddle boxes, built by Fairfield. This new vessel was a sister ship of the **Caledonia** (but with minor differences), built by Denny at Dumbarton in the same year.

J.N.

P.S. Marchioness of Breadalbane

In May 1889 The Caledonian Steam Packet Company was formed and registered as a limited company by the Directors of the Caledonian Railway, as they had failed to persuade any existing steamboat operator to provide a satisfactory connecting service for their trains to the new Gourock Pier. The Railway Company not being allowed, by law, to operate steamers, authorised its directors to purchase, on behalf of the new company, the two steamers **Madge Wildfire** and **Meg Merrilies** as well as the goodwill of the Dunoon and Kilmun service from the brothers Alec and Peter Campbell. The Campbells were happy to sell their Kilmun trade, as they had decided that the Bristol Channel now offered better prospects than the Clyde for an independent steamboat operator - with no railway fleet in competition. Thus began the famous Bristol Channel fleet of P. & A. Campbell. At the same time the new company took over the contracts for two new steamers which had been ordered by the Caledonian Railway (its parent company) in 1888. The first of these was the **Caledonia**, built by John Reid & Co., Port Glasgow and engined by Rankin & Blackmore (the builders of the present **Waverley**'s engine). On successful trials on 5 June 1889 **Caledonia** exceeded her guaranteed speed of 16.5 knots, and entered service on the Gourock - Rothesay run a few days later. She was an immediate success, and introduced many new features such as compound machinery and docking telegraphs.

The Caledonian Steam Packet Company ordered two more steamers in September 1889, to be repeats of the **Caledonia**; the first of these was the **Marchioness of Breadalbane**, launched by J. Reid & Co. on 15 April 1890 and named after the wife of the company's chairman. The only significant difference from the **Caledonia** was the placing of the bridge forward of the funnel, this became standard practice on subsequent ships. Speed was increased to 17 knots by increasing the boiler pressure to 100 lbs., the machinery again being constructed by Rankin & Blackmore. The new ship was elegantly fitted out, the main saloon and a

ladies cabin had the floors covered with Brussels carpets and runners; furnishings consisted of large sofas upholstered in high pile velvet, also a writing table and chairs. Dimensions of the '**Breadalbane**' and her sister ship the '**Marchioness of Bute**' were:- length 200.4ft., breadth 22.7ft. and depth 7.5ft. They could each carry 1119 passengers with a crew of 15. Machinery was compound but unusual in that the two cylinders were in tandem driving a single piston and connecting rod, instead of two separate ones as on the normal Clyde compound engine. There were two Navy boilers with a system of forced draught - hence the absence of large ventilators around the funnel.

The '**Breadalbane**' and the '**Bute**' were almost indistinguishable, but the rake of the funnel on the '**Bute**' was slightly more vertical. At the launch of the **Marchioness of Bute**, John Elder, the senior partner of the contractors Rankin & Blackmore, presided, and pointed out that the these steamers of the 1890's were much stronger and heavier than those of the 1860's and maintained speed with more comfort and seaworthiness. The '**Breadalbane**' was placed on the regular services from Wemyss Bay until called up for minesweeping duties in the first war, and based at Portsmouth. After the war she returned to Wemyss Bay, and was usually employed on the Millport run until the end of 1933, when she was transferred to Gourock for the Holy Loch run, on the disposal of **Caledonia**. She did this for one year only before being sold by the company to shipbreakers. However, this was not the end, as she was re-sold to the Redcliffe Shipping Co. Ltd. of Hull, who employed her on excursion work from Yarmouth and Lowestoft. In 1937 she was sold to German shipbreakers after a service of 47 years, 45 of which were with the Caledonian Company. Considering that she had been an all-the-year-round steamer her service was especially creditable. Her sister '**Marchioness of Bute**' had been sold by the Company for service on the Firth of Tay in 1908 and was broken up in 1923.

J.N.

P.S. "KENILWORTH"   J. NICHOLSON.

P.S. Kenilworth

The shipyard of A. & J. Inglis at Pointhouse on the east bank of the River Kelvin had a long association with the North British Railway Company and later the L.N.E.R. The company had built the first two North British steamers, the **Dandie Dinmont** and **Meg Merrilies** in 1866. Subsequently they had built the **Dandie Dinmont (II)** in 1895 and the **Talisman (I)** in 1896 when they received the order for the **Kenilworth,** virtually a repeat of the **Talisman (I)**. The **Kenilworth** was launched on 22 February 1898 and ran her trials on 30 June, when she attained a speed of 18.6 knots, slightly faster than the **Talisman**. Dimensions of the **Kenilworth** were:- length 215ft., breadth 23.lft., depth 7.6ft. and gross tonnage 333, later increased to 390. Resulting from the success of these two fine steamers, the Inglis yard received the contract for every subsequent North British and L.N.E.R. steamer with the exception of the Fairfield - built **Jeanie Deans** in 1931. The firm had been founded by the brothers Anthony and John Inglis in 1847, and at the time the **Kenilworth** was built the company was run by Dr John Inglis Jnr, son of Anthony Inglis and an outstanding designer of paddle steamers. He had studied both engineering and classics at Glasgow University, and in 1893 the University had conferred on him the honorary degree of Doctor of Law in recognition of his contribution to marine engineering and classics.

The **Kenilworth** and **Talisman** were driven by single cylinder diagonal engines, these caused a pulsating 'lurching' motion which some passengers found unpleasant. This type of engine also required great skill on the part of the engineer to ensure that the engine did not stall when the piston was at top dead centre. Also when leaving a pier both skill and hard work were required; I remember being on the **Eagle III** and watching with fascination as the engineer worked the valve control lever backwards and forwards as we left Kirn, carefully synchronising the movement of the lever with that of the huge crank. This

continued for some time until the ship was well under way and the eccentric valve control was able to take over, This process had to be repeated at every pier; I should imagine that the engineers always hoped for promotion or transfer to a steamer with compound engines!

Kenilworth and **Talisman** were employed on the Rothesay service from the North British base at Craigendoran, and both were called up for minesweeping duties in 1917, at first on the Clyde and later from Portsmouth. On release from war service they returned to the Rothesay and Kyles of Bute run; both had been noticeably altered; the **Kenilworth**'s bridge had been repositioned forward of the funnel in 1914 and the **Talisman**'s similarly whilst on war service. The fore saloon which originally had alleyways all round, had been extended to the full width of the hull, giving more space in the saloon and on the open deck above the saloon. Along with the other Craigendoran steamers, they became part of the L.N.E.R. fleet in 1923. Happily the old North British colours were retained by the L.N.E.R. - the only change was a new houseflag, a white St. Andrew's Cross on a dark blue background, with the letters L.N.E.R. in red on a central white oval. However in 1936 the L.N.E.R. adopted a drastic change of livery for their Clyde fleet. This consisted of a light grey hull with white deck houses, but by this time the **Talisman** had been scrapped and her place taken by a new **Talisman** - the diesel electric paddle vessel built by Inglis in 1935. However, the **Kenilworth** was first to appear in the new colour scheme from 1936 until she was withdrawn and broken up (by her builders) in 1938. It must be admitted that most people considered that these colours did not suit the Craigendoran steamers as well as did the original North British black hulls with brown-grained deck shelters and ventilators. Fortunately after the 1939 - 1945 war the L.N.E.R. reverted to the original N.B. colours, in which the new **Waverley** appeared in 1947.

J.N.

S.S. Dunara Castle

It is only within the last 50 years that David MacBrayne has had a monopoly of shipping services to the Western Isles. Previously the islands were served by several small companies. The original service from Glasgow to the Western Isles was provided by the ships of the Great West of Scotland Fishery Co. Ltd. When the company went out of business in 1860 its manager, Martin Orme, continued to operate its ships on his own behalf. Fifteen years later the trade had developed sufficiently for the company to order its fourth vessel - its third from the Port Glasgow yard of Blackwood and Gordon - in 1875. In the manner of the time, the hull was built of iron and the single screw was driven by a simple two cylinder engine which was compounded in 1882. The steamer was re-boilered in 1882 and again in 1894 when the original twin funnels were replaced by a single funnel, and it is in this form that she was best known. The vessel was named after a ruined castle on the north west coast of Mull.

The inhabitants of the Western Isles relied on the regular sailings from Glasgow round the Mull of Kintyre for their existence and down the years the **Dunara Castle** became a byword for regularity and reliability as she sailed among the islands with passengers and cargo. Even during both world wars she maintained her regular sailings despite the treacherous waters off the west coast being patrolled by German U-boats.

Ironically it was in peacetime that she suffered her two major mishaps - in August 1922 when she went aground at Battery Point, Greenock, and in March 1947 when she grounded at Bunessan. On this occasion she refloated successfully after a week ashore and continued on her voyage.

On 1 July 1929, Martin Orme & Co. Ltd. amalgamated with John McCallum & Co. Ltd. to become McCallum, Orme & Co. Ltd., and thereafter **Dunara Castle** sailed in consort with the other company's steamer, **Hebrides**. During the summer months the sailings were extended to include calls at the isolated St. Kilda groups sitting in the Atlantic some 40 miles west of North Uist. Indeed, one of **Dunara Castle's** principal claims to fame was her participation in the final evacuation of the remaining islanders in August 1930.

During the 1930's **Dunara Castle** sailed from Glasgow on a ten day frequency on either Monday or Thursday at 1515, and Greenock at 1915. After rounding the Mull, calls were made at Colonsay, Iona, Bunessan, Tiree, Elgol, Soay, Portnalong, Carbost, Struan, Poolteil, Dunvegan, Stein, Uig, Tarbert (Harris), Scalpay, Finsbay, Leverburgh, Lochmaddy, Kallin, Carnan (North Uist), Lochboisdale, Barra, Tiree, Bunessan, Iona and Colonsay. On occasions in summer the sailings were extended to St. Kilda or to Loch Roag on the north west coast of Lewis. The sailings were offered as cruises with full board for £10!

On 1 January 1948, the steamers of McCallum Orme were transferred to the fleet of David MacBrayne Ltd. following the takeover of the company. The cargo sailings were reorganized and **Dunara Castle** sailed from Glasgow on her last voyage on 19 January. On her return she was laid up in East India Harbour, Greenock, until April when she was towed to her birthplace at Port Glasgow for breaking up after 73 years of loyal service to the Western Isles.

After the withdrawal of **Dunara Castle** her calls were transferred to other ships of the fleet and chartering from other companies, principally J. & A. Gardner & Co. Ltd.. Also in 1949 regular services from Glasgow by sea to a number of destinations ceased. Substitution of road transport and transhipment also occurred where practicable. A replacement for **Dunara Castle** entered the MacBrayne fleet in 1949, a motor vessel built in Canada in 1946 and originally intended for war service, but sold to Dutch owners from whom she was purchased by Messrs. MacBrayne. After refitting at Irvine she was renamed **Loch Frisa,** after the largest inland loch on Islay, and sailed to the ports of the West Coast in consort with **Hebrides**. Following a further reorganisation of cargo services in 1953 this service was withdrawn and **Loch Frisa** served as spare vessel until sold in 1963 to Greek owners.

R.B.

S.S. Dalriada

The Campbeltown and Glasgow Steam Packet Joint Stock Co. Ltd. celebrated its centenary in 1926 by placing an order for a vessel with Messrs. Robert Duncan at Port Glasgow. A competition was held among the local schoolchildren to name the new steamer and **Dalriada** was selected for her launch on 16 March. A powerful triple expansion four cylinder engine, built by Messrs. David Rowan, drove a single screw to produce a speed of 18 knots on trial and earned her the title of the fastest single screw ship in the world.

During her first season she had regular races with the pioneer turbine steamer **King Edward**, and on her official trial trip on 30 April she sailed from Gourock to Campbeltown in under 3 hours to set a new record for this route. However, her entry into service was delayed by the aftermath of the General Strike and it was not until 28 June that she went into daily service sailing from Glasgow and Campbeltown on alternate days in consort with the veteran steamer **Davaar**. This was an all year round service and the extra tall funnel was fitted to provide natural draught for more economic sailing in the winter months.

Sailing from the Broomielaw, in the heart of Glasgow at 6 o'clock each morning, with calls at Greenock and Gourock, her route took her down-Firth round Garroch Head to call at Lochranza and Pirnmill (ferry) on Arran, and Carradale and Campbeltown on Kintyre. On special occasions the sailing was routed through the Kyles of Bute, and on local holidays she offered special sailings from Campbeltown to Tarbert Fair, Inveraray and Rothesay Illuminations. An annual sailing was given to Ayr in connection with the Ayr Show or Ayr Races. It was while on such a sailing on 28 April 1937 that she ran aground near Dunure in thick fog. She was successfully refloated by tugs and towed to Port Glasgow for repairs.

Shortly before this, the Campbeltown Company, in financial difficulties, had amalgamated with Clyde Cargo Steamers Ltd. to become the Clyde and Campbeltown Shipping Co. Ltd. The traditional Campbeltown funnel colours of black with a broad red band was replaced by MacBrayne red with a black top. In the summer of 1939, the company announced the withdrawal of **Davaar** leaving **Dalriada** to maintain the service with the cargo steamer **Ardyne**.

In January 1940, **Dalriada** was in collision with a destroyer and was withdrawn for repairs necessitating the re-commissioning of **Davaar** which closed the passenger service finally in March 1940. Thereafter, **Dalriada** was laid up in East India Harbour, Greenock, until requisitioned by the Admiralty in April 1940 when she was transferred to the Thames for duty as a salvage vessel to clear the wartime wrecks which were hindering navigation. While at anchor off Sheerness on 19 June 1942, having swung on the tide when she started her engines, she activated an acoustic mine under her stern and sank, fortunately without loss of life. Her wreck was blown up, in turn, in June 1946.

Until the building of an airfield at Machrihanish the **Davaar** and **Dalriada** provided the only reasonable means of travel to Campbeltown (though often not a comfortable journey in winter storms). Nevertheless it was usually preferable to the 150 mile road journey from Glasgow over the 'Rest and be Thankful'. Sadly the need for the ships disappeared with the regular air service for passengers from Glasgow, and a vast improvement in the A82 and A83 for heavy goods vehicles making the transport of cargo by road competitive despite the mileage. Now the only way one can enjoy a sail to Campbeltown is by the **Waverley**, once a week in July and August.

R.B.

T.S. Queen Alexandra (1912)

When the original turbine steamer of the name was badly damaged by fire while berthed in Greenock in September 1911 and subsequently sold to C.P.R., Capt. John Williamson ordered a replacement ship for his fleet of Turbine Steamers Ltd. from the yard of Messrs. William Denny at Dumbarton. At her launch on 8 April 1912 she was named **Queen Alexandra** and on trials on 18 May she recorded a speed of 21.5 knots which earned her builders and engineers a premium. With a length of over 270 feet and a certificate for 2160 passengers, she was the largest and the fastest of the Clyde turbine steamers and immediately became a great favourite with the travelling public.

She was placed on the excursion route from Greenock (Princes Pier) to Lochranza (Arran) and Campbeltown with calls at Gourock, Wemyss Bay and Fairlie and ferry calls at Pirnmill and Machrie Bay on Arran. Following the outbreak of war, she was requisitioned by the Admiralty in February 1915 for service as a troop transport sailing between Southampton and Le Havre. While on this service she made 668 voyages and carried a total of 353,038 officers and men. On three occasions she encountered U-Boats while on passage, the most dramatic of these being on 19 May 1918 when she rammed and sank the German submarine while travelling at full speed. Although considerably damaged by the impact, she reached Southampton safely. Capt. Angus Keith, her Master both on the Clyde and on naval service, was awarded an O.B.E. and D.S.C. for this exploit. Released by the Admiralty on 10 May 1919, she was reconditioned by Messrs. John Brown at Clydebank and returned to the Campbeltown service on 28 June.

The following year she changed routes with the turbine steamer **King Edward** and sailed daily from Greenock to Inveraray through the Kyles of Bute with calls at the Loch Fyne piers of Crarae and Strachur. In 1927 she was replaced on this service by the new turbine **King George V** and the **'Queen'** returned to the Campbeltown route although the call at Machrie ferry had been deleted.

The Turbine Steamers' summer season extended from May until September and by tradition the company opened its season with a cruise round Ailsa Craig which was frequently performed by **Queen Alexandra**. In June 1934 she gave the first ever Sunday sailing to Campbeltown sailing outward via Kilbrannan Sound and returning by Holy Isle, thus offering a cruise Round Arran.

She returned to the Inveraray service during the Glasgow Fair holiday each year and in July 1930 collided with the cargo steamer **Arran** off Ardlamont Point. The turbine was badly damaged at the water line at the bow but, by shepherding the passengers to the stern, she was able to return to Auchenlochan, to land the passengers, before going into dry dock for repairs.

In the spring of 1932 **Queen Alexandra** returned to her builders' yard at Dumbarton and reappeared with her promenade deck plated-in the length of the top deck and fitted with large observation windows and sliding embarkation doors after the manner of the newer turbines.

In October 1935 **Queen Alexandra** together with her consort **King George V** was purchased by Messrs. David MacBrayne Ltd. While she lay in Albert Harbour at Greenock the white funnels were repainted red. However the following spring she was taken in hand by Messrs. Lamont at Port Glasgow and re-emerged completely transformed with three funnels, a main mast and a new name - **Saint Columba**.

Apart from the war years, when she served as the Boom Defence Headquarters, while berthed in East India Harbour, Greenock, she maintained the Clyde section of the Royal Route from Glasgow and Greenock to Tarbert and Ardrishaig. She was finally withdrawn in September 1958 and towed to Port Glasgow for breaking up at the close of the year.

R.B.

T.S. Marchioness of Graham

When the C.S.P. Co. requested permission to order a further steam paddler in 1935, the L.M.S. Steam Vessels Committee insisted that competitive tenders be obtained for steam, diesel and turbine propulsion and subsequently the order was placed with the Fairfield Co. for a turbine steamer. Although laid down in September 1935 as **Glencloy**, that name was not available and the vessel was launched as **Marchioness of Graham** at Govan on 6 March 1936. The four turbines were geared to twin screws which produced a speed of 17.65 knots on trial on 8 April and made her the only geared turbine ship in the C.S.P. fleet. In service she replaced the former G.& S.W.R. turbine **Atalanta**, (to which she bore a considerable resemblance) as secondary Arran vessel and made her inaugural sailing on Friday 24 April. After a series of charters her first public sailing was on Sunday 7 June from Bridge Wharf to Lochgoilhead in place of **King Edward**.

Dimensions of the 'Graham' were: length 220ft, beam 30ft, depth 10ft. The open deck space behind the funnel was the first deliberate attempt on a Clyde Steamer to make provision for the conveyance of motor cars although boarding the vessel was a hazardous operation across two timber planks and depended on the state of the tide to enable the vessel's deck and the pier to be as level to each other as possible. Despite the travelling public's requirement to take cars on holiday, particularly to Arran, it was to be a further 17 years before the first purpose built car ferries were built for service on the Clyde.

Following the takeover of the Williamson-Buchanan fleet jointly by L.M.S. Railway and David MacBrayne in the autumn of 1935, the C.S.P. introduced a new fast service to Campbeltown from Ardrossan calling at Whiting Bay and taken by the turbine **Glen Sannox** thus the 'Graham' became principal Arran steamer Monday to Friday. She also inherited the traditional Glasgow Fair Friday evening sailing to Campbeltown, previously given by **Queen-Empress** or **Queen Alexandra**, now transferred to Adrossan and routed via Whiting Bay. In the winter months she maintained the combined Fairlie/Millport and Ardrossan/Arran service and in the summer of 1939, she frequently performed the "Fast Route" to Campbeltown.

During the war years she remained on the Clyde maintaining the Wemyss Bay/Millport/Kilchattan Bay service in summer and relieving to Rothesay or Arran during the winter. She also relieved the Holy Loch steamer each spring and autumn. In the summer of 1945 she gave Sunday cruises from Millport to Rothesay and the Kyles and the following winter maintained the Holy Loch service following the boiler failure of **Marchioness of Lorne**, until replaced in February 1946 by **Jupiter**, the first paddler to be reconditioned after war service. She returned to the Millport service in the summer of 1946 until replaced by **Duchess of Fife** in mid July and thereafter gave afternoon cruises. From 1946 she became winter steamer on the combined Fairlie/Millport/Arran service.

In 1947 she was based at Ayr for the resumption of the daily cruise programme giving relief sailings from Ardrossan to Whiting Bay on Saturdays. In 1952 calls at Troon were resumed. This programme continued until 1954 when she returned to the Arran service to replace the turbine **Glen Sannox** until herself replaced by the car ferry **Glen Sannox** in June 1957. By this time the 'Graham' was the last coal burning vessel in the C.S.P. fleet. She was surprisingly kept in steam for a programme of afternoon cruises and introduced the Up-River cruise from Largs to Bridge Wharf with late afternoon return down river. She was still required to provide an Ardrossan/Whiting Bay service on Saturdays. Following a breakdown to **Caledonia** she returned to Ayr briefly in mid summer. In 1956 she gave Sunday afternoon cruises from Gourock to Lochranza Bay or Round Holy Isle.

After being laid up in Albert Harbour throughout 1958 she was finally sold on 30th December for service in Greek waters providing cruises to the Aegean islands with a summer service from Genoa to the Balearics in 1966. She was laid up in Piraeus in 1968 and finally broken up a few years later.

R.B.

S.S. CHIEFTAIN

J. NICHOLSON

S.S. Chieftain

In 1907, the year that Mr. David MacBrayne died in his 93rd year, his elder son, Mr. David Hope MacBrayne, ordered a new vessel for the Glasgow - Stornoway route. The route had been operated for almost forty years by the **Clansman (II)**, built 1870, along with the **Claymore (I)** built 1881. The new vessel, launched at the Ailsa Shipbuilding Company's Ayr shipyard on 11 May 1907 by Mrs. D Hope MacBrayne and named **Chieftain**, was in effect a replacement for the elderly **Clansman**, which was sold in 1909 and broken up the following year. The **Chieftain** was a magnificent example of the shipbuilder's art, a vision of beauty, despite being in many respects a complete anachronism. She had a clipper bow, two tall masts and a single tall funnel, in appearance more like a yacht than a hard - working cargo and passenger vessel. The only other coastal vessel of similar yacht - like appearance was the even more anachronistic **St. Sunniva**, built in 1931 for the North of Scotland & Orkney & Shetland Steam Navigation Co. (the company to whom the **Chieftain** was eventually sold). The **St. Sunniva** looked even more yacht - like by having a tall cream/buff funnel with no black top. There is no doubt that the **Chieftain** was an outstanding ship, and despite her appearance had up to date luxury accommodation as befitted a vessel intended primarily for cruising. Her engines were triple expansion, built by the Clyde Shipbuilding & Engineering Co. at Port Glasgow, and her cargo handling was worked by modern silent electric winches. At 1080 gross tons with a length of 241ft. and beam 33ft. she was, at that time, the largest ship built for the company.

In the summer of 1907 she entered the company's service, sailing weekly from Glasgow to Stornoway in consort with the veteran **Claymore,** calling at the islands and piers of the west coast as far north as Ullapool before crossing the Minch to Stornoway, where she was long remembered with affection all along her route. However, she was not an unqualified success, cargo handling gear was not ideally designed for a trade with so many calls and she was a costly steamer to run.

Unfortunately, the passenger traffic on the route declined after a few years and, from 1909, **Chieftain** was normally only commissioned during the summer months. Following the Great War, the traffic was reduced to such an extent that one vessel was sufficient and the larger **Chieftain** was withdrawn and subsequently sold in 1919 to The North of Scotland & Orkney & Shetland Steam Navigation Co. Ltd. by whom she was renamed **St. Margaret**. The 'North' company, in turn, sold her to Canadian National Steamships Co. Ltd. in 1925, when she crossed the Atlantic for service in British Columbia and sailed under the name **Prince Charles**. Twenty years later she returned to the Mediterranean for service in Middle Eastern waters until finally broken up in 1952.

A magnificent ship, built in the flush of confidence, which suffered in time from the relentless advance of economics preventing her from becoming, in every sense, the Chieftain of the MacBrayne fleet.

R.B.

P.S. 'CHEVALIER' at OBAN   J. NICHOLSON.

P.S. Chevalier

In 1866 David Hutcheson & Co. ordered three vessels for their West Highland fleet from Messrs. Thomson at Govan. **Chevalier** was the largest, the other two being **Gondolier** and **Linnet**. The latter was a small screw steamer of 33 gross tons designed for the Crinan Canal on which she spent all of her long career. She was a small but important link in the Royal Route from Glasgow to Oban and the North. The **Gondolier** of 173 tons. was also built for canal work, but for the much longer Caledonian Canal, on which she sailed between Inverness and Banavie for over seventy years until withdrawn in 1939, having served through 4 reigns!

The **Chevalier** was much larger than the other two, with a gross tonnage of 292, a length of 211ft. and a beam of 22ft, being in effect a smaller edition of the third **Iona**, and was intended for the daily cruise from Oban round Mull to Staffa and Iona, on which she served for 20 years. She then transferred to the Corpach - Crinan service, which involved leaving her overnight berth at Banavie at the southern end of the Caledonian Canal at 0445. From Banavie she proceeded southwards to Fort William, with an intermediate call at Corpach, thence by Corran, Ballachulish, Appin and Lismore to Oban. After a brief call she continued by Easdale, Luing and Craignish to Crinan where her passengers were transferred to the little steamer **Linnet** for the sail along the canal to connect with the **Columba** at Ardrishaig. During her daily lay-up at Crinan between 1020 and 1500, advantage was taken to maintain the superlatively high standard associated with the MacBrayne steamers. From

mid-afternoon she retraced her route northwards calling at Oban at 1650 and Fort William at 1940 with the usual intermediate calls, until finally berthing at Banavie at 2010 - a working day of over 15 hours.

In 1886 the steamer's original horizontal boilers were replaced, and in 1901 she was again re-boilered, this time with two haystacks. In 1919 electric light was fitted and other improvements made to the accommodation.

Prior to the opening of the West Highland Railway to Fort William in 1894, **Chevalier** provided the principal means of communication with the south.

During the summers of 1913 and 1914, **Chevalier** maintained the Glasgow - Lochgoilhead service. She remained on the Clyde during the war years, for part of which she was on charter to C.S.P. Co. for service to Rothesay and to Millport from Wemyss Bay, still sailing with her MacBrayne red funnels.

The **Chevalier** usually laid up at Greenock in winter, but relieved on the Ardrishaig service when necessary, and it was on this service on 25 March 1927 that she suffered a paddle - wheel fracture in a gale, while on passage from Tarbert to Ardrishaig. The anchors did not hold, and she soon drifted on to rocks off Barmore Island. Boats were lowered, and 20 passengers, mail and luggage were brought safely ashore. After several days she proceeded to Greenock under her own steam, but examination showed that repair was not practicable and she was broken up at Troon after 61 years service.

R.B.

S.S. Claymore

When Mr David MacBrayne assumed full responsibility for the operations of David Hutcheson & Co in 1878, the first new steamer he ordered was the mighty **Columba** for the Glasgow - Ardrishaig section of the Royal Route to the Highlands. However the first ship ordered by him, when the company operated under his own name, was **Claymore** which, like **Columba** was a product of Messrs. Thomson's yard at Clydebank. Although launched on 14 July 1881 she did not run her trials until 1 October following which she went on to the Glasgow - Stornoway route which she was to serve all year round for the following 50 years.

With clipper bow, bowsprit and figurehead, twin masts fitted with derricks and gaffs and tall thin funnel, she was a perfectly proportioned example of high Victorian naval architecture. Her iron hull was driven by a two cylinder compound engine at a modest speed adequate for her service.

The **Claymore** sailed from Glasgow each Thursday afternoon at 1400, and from Greenock at 1800. Proceeding down-firth and rounding the Mull of Kintyre overnight she berthed at Oban at 0800 the following morning. From the "Charing Cross of the Highlands" her route took her up the sound of Mull with calls at Craignure, Lochaline, Salen and Tobermory. Continuing into the open waters and rounding Ardnamurchan Point, the most westerly projection of the British mainland, she proceeded to make calls at Eigg, Arisaig, Inverie, Armadale, Isle Oronsay, Glenelg, Balmacara, Kyleakin, Kyle of Lochalsh, Broadford and Portree where she was due to arrive in the early hours of Saturday morning. She then continued up the west coast of the mainland to Gairloch, Poolewe and Aultbea before finally crossing the Minch to berth at Stornoway at 1400 on Saturday afternoon.

After a Sabbath's rest at the Lewis capital she sailed early on Monday morning for Portree before retracing her route southward to arrive back in Glasgow at 0700 on Wednesday morning. There she would discharge her inboard cargo before reloading and setting off again on Thursday afternoon.

While this route was advertised as a tourist attraction during the summer months, with cabins and full board, she carried passengers all year round. Her mainstay was the cargoes and the basic necessities of life, which she carried to the many islands and isolated communities of the west coast, prior to the opening of land communication with the development of road and rail transport. On her inward sailings she carried livestock and local produce to the markets in the south.

Summer and winter, **Claymore** navigated the treacherous waters off the west coast, in fair weather and foul, until May 1931 when she was sold for breaking up. Her last sailing was up the west coast and round the north of Scotland to her final resting place, in the breakers yard, at Bo'ness on the Forth.

It is not generally appreciated, in these days, how much the inhabitants of the remote towns and villages, of the islands and west coast of Scotland, depended on ships like the **Claymore** for the very necessities of life. The sea, of course was the only means of access for the islands and many places on the mainland and the arrival of the steamer, usually twice weekly, was the highlight of the week. This is still the case at many places on the west coast of Norway, where a vessel leaves Bergen each evening for the long voyage to the 'Land of the midnight sun,' with numerous calls at remote villages similar to those on **Claymore**'s weekly voyage to the north. In both Norway and Scotland navigating between the islands in all kinds of weather, mostly in darkness in winter, demanded a high degree of skill and local knowledge on the part of the officers and crew, without the help of modern aids such as radar, sonar and radio direction finders. It is a tribute to their competence that there were so few accidents.

R.B.

P.S. "FUSILIER" OBAN   J. NICHOLSON

P.S. Fusilier

When Mr David MacBrayne decided to add a new paddle steamer to his fleet in 1888, he accepted the tender submitted by Messrs. Hutson & Corbett, engineers in Glasgow who subcontracted the building of the vessel to Messrs. John McArthur & Co Ltd. at the yard on the banks of the River Cart in Paisley. With a clipper bow, figurehead and bowsprit, the new steamer bore a close resemblance to **Grenadier**, three years her senior.

The **Fusilier's** dimensions were: length 202ft. breadth 21.6ft. depth 8.1ft. and gross tonnage 251. Machinery was a single cylinder diagonal engine giving a nominal horsepower of 133. This was in contrast to the old oscillating machinery of earlier MacBrayne ships, but it seems surprising that a single cylinder engine was installed, after the previous vessel - **Grenadier** - had compound machinery. So the **Fusilier** suffered from the usual pulsating motion inherent in this type of machinery. Her original haystack boiler was replaced in 1901.

The little paddler had a varied career in the MacBrayne fleet and, in the summer months, was usually based at Oban from where she sailed north to Corpach to connect with the company's steamers on Loch Ness, sailing to Inverness and calling en route at Fort William to connect with the West Highland Railway. She also served on the Oban - Crinan route linking through the canal with the **Columba** at Ardrishaig and frequently gave short excursion sailings out of Oban.

During the first war, **Fusilier** provided sailings from Glasgow to Kirn and Dunoon during the summer of 1916 and later was chartered by the Caledonian Steam Packet Company principally for the service from Wemyss Bay to Rothesay when her red funnel was repainted in "Caley" yellow.

Following the loss of **Grenadier** by fire at Oban in September 1927, **Fusilier** took over her services, sailing to Staffa and Iona in the summer months, and maintaining the Clyde service between Greenock and Ardrishaig during the winter. While being overhauled in the spring of 1928, the bridge was moved forward of the funnel which was extended by the depth of the black top.

A new deckhouse was built over the main companionway on the promenade deck and new sponson houses were added aft. The **Fusilier** usually spent the winter laid up at Greenock or Bowling. She was the last vessel built for the company in the 19th century

When she was replaced by **Lochfyne** at Oban in 1931, **Fusilier** transferred to the Skye mail service giving a return sailing daily from Portree to Kyle and Mallaig in succession to the veteran **Glencoe**. In 1934 she was replaced in turn by the new **Lochnevis** and was laid up at Ardrossan until sold for cruising from Granton on the Firth of Forth. She was soon found to be too extravagant on fuel for this work, and was re-sold for service in North Wales, renamed **Lady Orme**, after the headland at the western end of Llandudno Bay. She was given a white hull and the pale yellow funnel of the Liverpool and North Wales Steamship Company. This company was closely associated with the Fairfield shipyard who had built a number of their steamers, culminating in the last two - the superb **St Tudno** (2,300 gross tons) in 1926 and **St Seiriol** in 1931 for their main Liverpool - Llandudno - Menai Bridge service. During 1936 the **Lady Orme** cruised out of Ramsgate before returning to North Wales when she was given her third name: **Crestawave**. Eventually she was laid up in Liverpool and later at Barrow until broken up in 1939.

I.Q.

T.S. 'KING GEORGE V'   J. NICHOLSON

T.S. King George V

Few steamers which have sailed the waters of the Clyde and the Western Isles have been as revolutionary or as trendsetting as **King George V**, built by William Denny & Bros. Ltd. at Dumbarton in 1926. She had an enclosed promenade deck containing an observation saloon forward and sliding embarkation doors amidships. A spacious dining saloon with large windows was located aft on the main deck instead of being at a lower level with portholes on the water line.

Even more revolutionary was the engine room below, where the twin screws were driven by high pressure turbines fed with superheated steam at 750º F producing a pressure of 550 lbs. giving a speed on trials of 20.78 knots.

The steamer entered service on 8 September 1926, and from 1927 onwards, **King George V** served as the regular Inveraray steamer based at Greenock (Princes Pier), and calling at Gourock, Dunoon, Rothesay, Tighnabruaich, Crarae and Strachur, and offering one hour ashore at Inveraray before retracing her route. In midsummer season she provided a programme of evening cruises in consort with **Queen Alexandra**.

While the steamer was sailing to Irvine for winter lay-up in September 1927, a steam tube burst severely scalding two firemen who later died after being rescued from the stokehold.

The steamer was re-boilered in 1929 when navy tops were added to the funnels and the lifeboats, originally amidships, were repositioned aft on the upper deck. Shortly after this, another boiler tube burst while the ship was in the Kilbrannan Sound en route to Campbeltown, but she returned to Wemyss Bay under reduced power and disembarked the passengers. Finally, in 1935, it was decided to replace the high pressure boilers with one double ended Scotch boiler working at a "normal" pressure of 200 lbs. New funnels of larger diameter were fitted.

King George V and **Queen Alexandra** regularly exchanged routes and it is ironic that, under these circumstances, each vessel was damaged in collision. On 7 August 1934, **King George V** was in collision with the L.N.E.R. paddler **Jeanie Deans** off Garroch Head, but continued to Campbeltown.

On Friday 10 July 1931, the turbine was chartered to carry their Majesties King George V and Queen Mary to the opening of the new dock at Shieldhall which His Majesty named King George V Dock.

In October 1935, the fleets of Williamson - Buchanan Steamers Ltd. and Turbine Steamers Ltd. were jointly purchased by L.M.S. Railway Company and David MacBrayne Ltd. with the turbine steamers becoming MacBrayne ships. In November, **King George**'s funnels were repainted red, and the following spring she was fitted with additional lifeboats in preparation for her new service, based at Oban, sailing daily round Mull on the Sacred Isle Cruise to Staffa and Iona. She continued to carry out this sailing until finally withdrawn in September 1974.

King George V was requisitioned by the Admiralty in January 1940 for service as a troop transport based at Dover. In May she was dispatched to Dunkirk and made five trips into the harbour under enemy gunfire, and was one of the last vessels to leave. Thereafter, she was based at Gourock for tender duties.

After reconditioning at Dumbarton, she maintained the Clyde service from Gourock to Tarbert and Ardrishaig in 1946, returning to Oban in 1947. At this time, her embarkation doors were stained and varnished and were not repainted white until 1950. A wheelhouse was fitted in 1948 and she carried a mainmast from 1952. In June 1957, she ran aground on Scarba in thick fog while en route to Oban, but was successfully refloated after being in danger of capsizing.

After her final sailings from Oban to Iona on 14 September 1974, and on charter to Loch Sunart the following day, she was laid up in Greenock until April 1975 when she was sold and towed to Cardiff where she was laid up. In the spring of 1981, she was re-sold to become a floating restaurant but was severely damaged by fire while conversion was underway, and was finally beached at the mouth of the River Taff - an inglorious end to a steamer which was unique in the affection in which she was held, in both Clyde and West Highland waters.

R.B.

T.S. DUCHESS OF HAMILTON.   J. NICHOLSON

T.S. Duchess of Hamilton

Taking advantage of the competitive prices for new ships during the depression years, and following the outstanding success and popularity of the turbine steamer **Duchess of Montrose**, built by Denny Bros. in 1930, the L.M.S. Railway Company authorised its subsidiary, the Caledonian Steam Packet Company, to order a similar vessel to replace the 1898 **Juno** on the excursion programme based at Ayr. The successful tender was submitted by Messrs. Harland and Wolff at Govan and the engines were built in the company's engine shops at Belfast. The steamer was launched on the 5 May 1932 by the Duchess of Hamilton herself, and went on trials on 24 June, when she achieved a speed of 20.65 knots.

With a length of 262ft. and beam of 32ft. she was 2ft. longer than the '**Montrose**', but her hull form was quite different, the hull of '**Montrose**' being more like that of the **King George V**. Other differences from the '**Montrose**' were the window arrangements on the main deck, slightly narrower funnels with shallower black top, and the fitting of a bow rudder, and later a cross-trees on the mainmast. Both ships were triple-screw, with the turbines directly coupled to the three propeller shafts, as on the earlier turbine steamers prior to **King George V**. The '**Hamilton**' and the '**Montrose**' were designed as one class ships; by not having to duplicate facilities for two classes, more space was provided in the public areas. The spaciousness was particularly apparent in the observation saloon at the forward end of the superstructure, within which attractive twin stairs from port and starboard sides joined into a single central stairway down to the main deck, leading to a very comfortably furnished lounge with armchairs and tables and small curtained windows - a most welcoming room if the weather was cold or raining!

The observation saloon was furnished with Lloyd Loom chairs, and abaft the twin stairways was a space which housed a piano and was a favourite venue for the steamer's band to entertain the passengers.

In July 1932, the new **Duchess** cruised out of Ayr, Troon and Ardrossan to such varied destinations as Lochgoilhead, Campbeltown, Inveraray, Girvan and round Ailsa Craig. With the outbreak of war in 1939, she was requisitioned by the Admiralty, but remained in home waters, to serve as a tender on the Clyde carrying troops from the railheads at Gourock and Greenock (Princes Pier) to the ships assembling in convoy at the "Tail of the Bank". There were considerable troop movements between Scotland and Ulster, and **Duchess of Hamilton** served as a transport between Stranraer and Larne. It was while on this service that she grounded on Corsewall Point in thick fog in December 1945 and severely damaged her bow.

After she was successfully refloated, she was "demobbed" and reconditioned to return to pleasure sailings and to a new service based at Gourock sailing to Campbeltown and Inveraray on alternate days. On 1 June 1946, she gave the first passenger sailing to Campbeltown since 1939 and received a civic reception. Later her service was extended to include weekly sailings to Arran via the Kyles, and to Ayr with an afternoon cruise round Holy Isle. It was while on the Ayr sailings on Friday mornings that she had weekly races with **Duchess of Montrose** (on the Campbeltown service) between Rothesay and Largs.

During overhaul in the spring of 1956, the **Duchess** was converted to burn oil fuel, and radar was fitted in 1960. In 1969, in company with most of the Clyde fleet, her masts were truncated to enable her to sail under the Kingston Bridge - an alteration which destroyed, completely, her profile.

Of the eight Captains of the **Hamilton**, three were well known to regular passengers and steamer enthusiasts - Fergus Murdoch, James Findlay and David McCormick. Captain Murdoch, or 'Fergie' as he was generally referred to, was her Master for 21 summers 1947 - 1967, and took his favourite vessel to her final lay-up berth in 1970. The '**Hamilton**' will long be remembered by the public and shiplovers who to this day recall with affection the many happy days spent on board this fine ship.

She was withdrawn from service in September 1970 and laid up in East India Harbour in Greenock. After a futile attempt to convert her to a floating restaurant, the Clyde's last **Duchess** was towed to Troon for breaking up in April 1974.

I.Q.

D.E.V. 'LOCHFYNE'   J. NICHOLSON

D.E.V. Lochfyne

When the L.M.S. Railway Company and Coast Lines Ltd. jointly acquired David MacBrayne & Co Ltd. in 1928, they inherited a fleet of ageing and obsolete ships which they set about replacing with modern tonnage. The contrast could not have been greater with several of the older steam vessels replaced by diesel engined ships. As a replacement for **Grenadier**, which had been broken up after being badly damaged by fire at Oban in 1927, they placed an order with Denny at Dumbarton for a twin screw vessel driven by diesel electric engines supplied by Davey Paxman & Co Ltd. of Colchester. At her launch on 20 March in 1931, she was named **Lochfyne** and, on trials, attained a speed of over 16 knots which was adequate for her proposed services. It would be difficult to imagine a greater contrast between the older members of the fleet and this smart new motor vessel with two short funnels with horizontal tops, solid bulwarks forward of an observation saloon on the covered promenade deck, and cruiser stern.

In June 1931, she arrived at Oban to take up her station on the Sacred Isle Cruise round Mull to Staffa and Iona. From October until April each year she maintained the company's winter service on the Clyde between Greenock and Ardrishaig and, with her central heating, was well equipped for winter sailing. During the early months her hull was painted grey, but was black from October.

With the advent of the turbine steamer **King George V** at Oban in June 1936, **Lochfyne** became secondary Oban steamer but not before both ships had sailed on charter to Iona in a symbolic hand over of the route.

For the following four summers **Lochfyne** maintained the Oban - Fort William service and operated day excursions out of Oban until July 1939 when, while berthed at the North Pier, an explosion in her starboard engine caused considerable damage. The stricken vessel was able to make her own way to Greenock for repairs but it was not until March 1940 that she was ready to return to service. With the intervening outbreak of war and the

laying of the Cloch - Dunoon boom, she was based at Wemyss Bay for the Tarbert and Ardrishaig mail service which she maintained throughout the war years. In June 1945, she was the first Clyde steamer to be repainted in peacetime colours by a gradual process while berthed overnight at Wemyss Bay, with the result that she sailed with the stern half and second funnel in full colour while the bow section and forward funnel were still grey.

In June 1946, **Lochfyne** returned to Oban to operate single-handed on alternate days to Staffa and Iona or to Fort William, until the return of **King George V** in 1947, when she operated a programme of day excursions, including regular sailings from Oban to Islay.

Lochfyne was re-engined in 1953 with British Polar diesels and, at the same time, was fitted with a mainmast.

When **Saint Columba** was withdrawn from service in September 1958, **Lochfyne** became the Ardrishaig mail steamer all year round, although subsequently her winter sailings were terminated at Tarbert. Each year she paid a brief visit to Oban in May to open the summer excursion programme. In order to provide adequate deck accommodation amidships for the stowing of mailbags, the staircase was refitted at the rear of the extended upper deck.

With the creation of the Scottish Transport Group in 1969 and its subsequent takeover of David MacBrayne Ltd., it was decided to withdraw the MacBrayne Clyde service. **Lochfyne** gave the last sailing to Ardrishaig on 13 September and to Tarbert on 30 September 1969 when she ended a tradition of 116 years of Clyde sailings.

An early proposal for conversion to a floating restaurant failed to materialise and she became an accommodation ship for Metal Industries Ltd. berthed alongside their shipbreaking yard at Faslane in the Gareloch. After being laid up in Stephen's basin at Govan in 1972 **Lochfyne** was finally towed to Dalmuir for breaking up in 1974.

I.Q.

P.S. Mountaineer

P.S. Mountaineer, the last paddle steamer to be constructed for the West Highland fleet of David MacBrayne, was a step backwards in design. She had a low open bow and fore saloon in the Victorian style although she was built in 1910, five years after the **Pioneer** which had a built up bow. Both ships were products of Messrs. Inglis yard at Pointhouse on the banks of the River Kelvin and were fitted with the small paddlewheels and resultant small paddleboxes typical of the period. Originally, **Mountaineer** was boarded to the level of the handrail around the fore end of the promenade deck in an attempt to provide protection to passengers but, as this resulted in considerable resistance in strong winds and rough seas, it was removed after a few years.

The **Mountaineer**'s dimensions were: length 180ft. beam 20ft. depth 7.7ft. and gross tonnage 235. Despite being 20ft. longer than the **Pioneer**, built at the same yard in 1905, her tonnage was 6 tons less than the earlier ship, probably due to the promenade deck not extending to the bow; in many respects she was a retrograde step in design. The large windows below the forward end of the promenade deck enclosed a 3rd. class saloon. Machinery was a compound diagonal engine of 86 registered H.P.

When she entered the company's service, **Mountaineer** was placed on the Oban - Crinan service in succession to **Chevalier** She was based at Oban each summer and regularly maintained the Oban - Fort William service and also gave regular excursion sailings up the Sound of Mull to Tobermory. Later she also maintained a ferry service between Oban and Lismore. Indeed, the little paddler was a "maid of all work" and relieved regularly on the Islay mail service and, from time to time, operated between Mallaig and Portree.

On the Clyde she regularly relieved on the mail service from Greenock to Lochgoilhead. **Mountaineer** was not required for war service and spent several of the war years on charter to the North British Co to maintain the Gareloch sailings from Craigendoran and Helensburgh.

The smart little paddler proved to be a reliable member of the MacBrayne fleet but, with the renewal of the fleet with the introduction of new motor ships during the 1930's, she became surplus to requirements and, in 1938, was sold for breaking up at Port Glasgow after 28 years sailing under the MacBrayne pennant - a short life by that company's standards. Although similar to the **Pioneer** of 1905, she was not as good-looking nor as long-lived as the **Pioneer**, which was not scrapped until 1958.

I.Q.

P.S. Pioneer (1905)

The first MacBrayne paddle steamer to be built by Messrs. Inglis at Pointhouse was the **Pioneer**, a trim little ship decked to the bow but retaining the bridge behind the funnel and between the paddle boxes in the traditional manner. She was launched in February 1905 and ran her trials on 25 March when a speed of 14 knots was recorded - sufficient for the Islay mail service for which she was designed. The compound diagonal engine drove small paddle wheels after the current fashion with the result that the paddle boxes were level with the handrail around the promenade deck.

The paddle boxes also differed from the rest of the MacBrayne fleet in that the fan-vents were horizontal slots instead of the standard radial type. A haystack boiler (chosen to reduce weight and hence draught) supplied steam at 120lbs. pressure. **Pioneer**'s dimensions were: length 160ft. beam 22ft. depth 8.3ft. and gross tonnage 241.

In April 1905 when she took over the route which she was to make her own for the following 35 years, replacing the veteran paddler **Glencoe**, the contrast could not have been greater. Based on Islay at Port Ellen or Port Askaig on alternate nights, she worked into West Loch Tarbert calling at Gigha on Port Ellen sailings and at Craighouse (Jura) when inward bound from Port Askaig. After discharging her passengers to make the short overland journey to Tarbert pier on Loch Fyne, she reloaded and returned to Islay.

During the years she became a well loved and reliable ship serving the southernmost islands of the Inner Hebrides, summer and winter, with only a brief spell off duty for her annual overhaul.

When she was due to be replaced by the new motor vessel **Lochiel** in 1939, it was found that the depth of the new ship was too great to allow her to berth in the shallow waters of West Loch Tarbert until dredging operations had been undertaken, and so the paddler continued in service for a further year. Eventually, in 1941, she was replaced by the new ship and transferred north to relieve on the Tobermory mail service from Oban, and to Portree from Mallaig and Kyle.

In 1943 she was laid up until acquired by the Admiralty in 1944. Moored off Fairlie she served as HQ ship for the North Atlantic submarines. After the war she was purchased by the Admiralty and renamed **HMS Harbinger** for service at Portland Harbour until 1958 when she was sold for breaking up.

There was an earlier **Pioneer**, built in 1844 for the Glasgow, Paisley & Greenock Railway Company, acquired by J. & G. Burns in 1847 and transferred to Messrs. Hutcheson in 1851. They employed her on the Glasgow - Ardrishaig summer service, and later on services from Oban. She formed part of the Royal Route, which originally commenced at Glasgow. This involved several steamers, the Crinan Canal track-boat, a coach from Corpach to Banavie, and a steamer to Inverness.

A third **Pioneer** was built by Messrs. Henry Robb at Leith in 1974. A twin screw passenger and car ferry with bridge control of diesel engines she was designed specifically for the Islay service from West Loch Tarbert with reduced depth to operate in its shallow waters. In recent years she has seen service on many West Highland routes and in summer months is the regular vessel on the Wemyss Bay - Rothesay service while also giving day cruises to Brodick (Arran).

I.Q.

P.S. Duchess of Rothesay

Reported by many as the Caledonian Steam Packet Company's classic paddle steamer, **Duchess of Rothesay** was typical of the many outstanding products from the yard of Messrs. Thomson at Clydebank where she was launched in April 1895. On her trials on 17 May, she recorded 18.10 knots, and was reported to have cost over £20,000. With her long slender hull and tall funnel at a jaunty rake, she earned herself the title "the Cock of the Walk". With dimensions of 225.6ft. x 26.1ft. x 8.6ft. the 'Rothesay' was slightly smaller than her rival 'Jupiter'

When placing the order in December 1894 Capt. James Williamson said he wanted a fast boat with reliable machinery and fitted with the best accommodation. So, compound two-crank engines were installed and a double-ended Scotch boiler rather than the Navy type used on the company's previous new ships. She was fitted out as a smaller version of the pride of the fleet, the luxurious **Duchess of Hamilton**. Captain Donald McPhedran, one of the most popular "Caley" masters of the nineties took out the new ship, and from the start she was a winner and, during her lifetime of over 50 years, proved to be one of the most successful of Clyde steamers.

The new paddler was placed on the Gourock - Rothesay service after initially sailing between Ardrossan and Arran. However, in 1897 she replaced the **Ivanhoe** on the Arran via the Kyles service on which she sailed in direct competition with the G. & S.W.R. paddler **Jupiter** which had been built at Clydebank in 1896 especially for this route. For the following ten summers these two perfectly matched classic paddle steamers vied with each other as they raced daily through the Kyles of Bute before calling at Corrie (ferry), Brodick, Lamlash, Kingscross (ferry) and Whiting Bay, the latter also a ferry call until the pier was opened in 1899.

The **"Duchess"** carried illustrious royal namesakes – the Prince and Princess of Wales when they opened Rothesay Dock at Clydebank in 1907, and the King and Queen when they visited Beardmore's yard at Dalmuir in 1914.

With the outbreak of war and the laying of the anti-submarine boom between the Cloch and Dunoon, the paddler was based at Wemyss Bay for the Rothesay service until she was taken over by the Admiralty, in 1915, to serve as a minesweeper based at Sheerness and later Portland. While minesweeping she towed a disabled zeppelin into Margate, and assisted in the salvage of 15 ships and swept up more than five hundred mines without harm to herself.

On her return to the Clyde, in April 1919, she was berthed up-river at Merklands Wharf where she sank on 1 June after a seacock had been inadvertently left open.

However, she was raised successfully and reconditioned to return to peacetime service, in March 1920, when she was placed on the Kyles of Bute service from Greenock (Princes Pier) and Gourock. From 1926 this involved leaving Rothesay (where she lay overnight) at 7.10am for Wemyss Bay, thence on to Greenock Princes Pier, which she left again at 10.25am for all piers to Auchenlochan. After a brief stay there she retraced her route to Princes Pier, ready to take the express train connection to Dunoon at 4.45pm, then back to Gourock for another run to Dunoon and back again to Gourock for a final run to Rothesay, where she finished her day's work at about 9pm - 13 hours with hardly a break all day!

Acquired for a second period of war service in 1939, she was converted once again for minesweeping and took part in the withdrawal from Dunkirk. Later she served as an accommodation ship at Harwich. In 1946 it was not considered economic to recondition the 51 year old paddler and she was towed to Belgium for breaking up.

I.Q.

P.S. 'WAVERLEY' (1899 - 1940)   J. NICHOLSON.

P.S. Waverley (1899)

One of the most outstanding ships of the North British Company's fleet of paddle steamers was **Waverley** which was built and engined by Messrs. A & J Inglis at Pointhouse in 1899. The largest member of the north-bank based fleet, she had a low bow and extended fore saloon with the mast fitted on the promenade deck. The tall well raked funnel and the bridge between the paddle boxes completed a graceful outline. The railway company abandoned its previous conservative policy by agreeing to the installation of the first set of compound diagonal engines in the fleet, with the twin cranks driving the ship at over 19 knots to make her a fit rival to the south-bank fliers of the C.S.P. and G. & S.W.R. fleets.

Originally, the new ship was placed on the excursion sailings from Craigendoran to such destinations as Ayr, Campbeltown and Inveraray but, with the winding up of the North British Steam Packet Company in 1902, her railway ownership restricted her area of operations and she cruised round Bute.

In November 1915, the Admiralty acquired **Waverley** and had the promenade deck extended to the bow which was built up for service as a minesweeper based on the east and south coasts of England. On her return from war service, the built up bow was retained and the bridge was moved forward of a new larger funnel. In 1920 she was placed on the service to Lochgoilhead and Arrochar as the Clyde section of the "Three Lochs Tour" which was probably the most popular day excursion on the Clyde, especially with English and overseas visitors to Rothesay and Dunoon. On leaving the **Waverley** at Arrochar they were able to walk or bus across to Tarbet, then sail down Loch Lomond to Balloch, where a steam train was waiting to take them to Craigendoran to rejoin the **Waverley** for the return journey. This tour was restored after 1947 with a new **Waverley**, and in May 1953 the new paddle steamer **Maid Of The Loch** took over the Loch Lomond part of the tour. During the summer of 1931 she was replaced on this route by **Jeanie Deans** but, when the new paddler was transferred to a new programme of day cruises in 1932, **Waverley** resumed the Arrochar service.

When the North British Railway became part of the L.N.E.R. group in 1923, there was no obvious alteration to its Clyde fleet. However, in 1934, deck saloons were fitted to the **Waverley** and, in 1936, she was repainted in the new L.N.E.R. livery of grey hull and white deck saloons but retained the traditional tricolour funnel.

With the withdrawal of cruises and the general reduction in L.N.E.R. Clyde sailings in 1938, **Jeanie Deans** returned to Lochgoilhead and Arrochar, and **Waverley** took the afternoon sailing to the Kyles of Bute for what was to prove her last season of service on the Clyde. Laid up in Bowling harbour, the old paddler was destined for the shipbreakers, however the outbreak of war in September 1939 resulted in a reprieve, when she was hurriedly re-commissioned, to help in the evacuation of children from Glasgow to the Clyde coast. In October, she was acquired by the Admiralty for a second period of naval duty as a minesweeper. In May 1940 she was sent across the Channel to assist in the evacuation of Dunkirk. On her return, laden with British troops rescued from the beaches, she was repeatedly attacked by German bombers. Despite shooting down two of the enemy aircraft, her steering gear was put out of action and the disabled ship received a direct hit as a result of which she sank with loss of life but with most of her complement rescued.

Capt. John Cameron, **Waverley**'s Clyde skipper in the 1930's went to war with her, and stepped off the bridge into the sea as she went down. He was awarded D.S.C. and D.S.O. for his gallantry in this action. In 1947 Capt. Cameron commissioned the new **Waverley** and in later years was an advocate for and an active supporter of her preservation. In 1980 and again in 1990 **Waverley** sailed in the wake of her illustrious predecessor in commemoration of Dunkirk.

The 1899 **Waverley** in her 1920 - 34 condition was the best looking and probably the most popular steamer of the Craigendoran fleet. A brass porthole, salvaged from her wreck, is on display in the Clyde Room at Glasgow's Transport Museum.

I.Q.

CONSIGN "PER McCALLUM, ORME & CO., LTD. STEAMERS."

SUMMER SAILINGS, 1939
GLASGOW
AND THE
WEST HIGHLANDS

THE UNDERNOTED OR OTHER STEAMERS ARE INTENDED TO SAIL WITH GOODS AND PASSENGERS
As under (until further notice, and unless prevented by any unforeseen circumstances)

| FROM GLASGOW AT 3.15 P.M. | FROM GREENOCK AT 7.15 P.M. Except "CHALLENGER" |

"HEBRIDES"
LOADING BERTH, 46 LANCEFIELD QUAY.
(Telephone CENTRAL 0221)
Calling at **Custom House Quay, Greenock.**

THURSDAY,	30th	MARCH
TUESDAY,	11th	APRIL
THURSDAY,	20th	APRIL
MONDAY,	1st	MAY
THURSDAY,	11th	MAY
MONDAY,	22nd	MAY
THURSDAY,	1st	JUNE
MONDAY,	12th	JUNE
THURSDAY,	22nd	JUNE
MONDAY,	3rd	JULY
THURSDAY,	13th	JULY
MONDAY,	24th	JULY
THURSDAY,	3rd	AUGUST
MONDAY,	14th	AUGUST
THURSDAY,	24th	AUGUST
MONDAY,	4th	SEPTEMBER
THURSDAY,	14th	SEPTEMBER
MONDAY,	25th	SEPTEMBER

Calling at—
Bonahaven for Portàskaig, Colonsay, Oban, Tobermory, Coll, Tiree, Barra, Castlebay (Northbay), Lochboisdale, Skipport, Carnan, Scotvin (Kallin), Locheport, Lochmaddy, Tarbert (Harris), Uig, Dunvegan (Colbost), Pooltiel, *Struan, Carbost, Coll, Tiree, *Tobermory, Oban, Colonsay, Portaskaig.
* No Call at Struan on Thursday Sailings.
* No call at Tobermory coming South on Aug. 31st & Sept. 21st.

"DUNARA CASTLE"
LOADING BERTH, 46 LANCEFIELD QUAY.
(Telephone CENTRAL 0221)
Calling at West Quay, Greenock.

MONDAY,	3rd	APRIL
THURSDAY,	13th	APRIL
MONDAY,	24th	APRIL
THURSDAY,	4th	MAY
MONDAY,	15th	MAY
THURSDAY,	25th	MAY
MONDAY,	5th	JUNE
THURSDAY,	15th	JUNE
MONDAY,	26th	JUNE
THURSDAY,	6th	JULY
MONDAY,	17th	JULY
THURSDAY,	27th	JULY
MONDAY,	7th	AUGUST
THURSDAY,	17th	AUGUST
MONDAY,	28th	AUGUST
THURSDAY,	7th	SEPTEMBER
MONDAY,	18th	SEPTEMBER
THURSDAY,	28th	SEPTEMBER

Calling at—
Colonsay, Iona, Bunessan, Tiree, Elgoll, Soay, Portnalong, Carbost, Struan, Pooltiel, Dunvegan (Colbost), Stein, Uig, Tarbert (Harris), Scalpay, Finsbay, Leverburgh, Lochmaddy, Kallin (Scotvin), Carnan, Lochboisdale, Barra, Castlebay (Northbay), Tiree, Bunessan, Iona, Colonsay.

"CHALLENGER"
(WITH CARGO ONLY)
LOADING BERTH, 6 KINGSTON DOCK.
(Telephone SOUTH 880)

THURSDAY,	6th	APRIL
MONDAY,	17th	APRIL
THURSDAY,	27th	APRIL
MONDAY,	8th	MAY
THURSDAY,	18th	MAY
MONDAY,	29th	MAY
THURSDAY,	8th	JUNE
MONDAY,	19th	JUNE
THURSDAY,	29th	JUNE
MONDAY,	10th	JULY
THURSDAY,	20th	JULY
MONDAY,	31st	JULY
THURSDAY,	10th	AUGUST
MONDAY,	21st	AUGUST
THURSDAY,	31st	AUGUST
MONDAY,	11th	SEPTEMBER
THURSDAY,	21st	SEPTEMBER
MONDAY,	2nd	OCTOBER

Calling at—
Iona, Bunessan, Barra, Castlebay (Northbay), Eriskay, Lochboisdale, Skipport, Carnan, Petersport, Locheport, Lochmaddy, Leverburgh, Tarbert (Harris), Scalpay, Uig.

AND ANY OTHER PORTS THAT MAY BE AGREED UPON.
" HEBRIDES " leaves OBAN going North on the day after leaving Glasgow not before 1 p.m., and leaves OBAN again when coming South not before 1 p.m. on April 5th, 17th and 26th. May 6th, 17th and 29th. June 8th, 19th and 27th. July 10th, 20th and 31st. August 10th, 21st and 31st. September 11th and 21st.

PASSENGER FARES TO OR FROM GLASGOW, SINGLE JOURNEY.

	*Cabin	Steerage		*Cabin	Steerage
BONAHAVEN FOR PORTASKAIG, ISLAY	17/3	9/3	KALLIN via Harris	60/3	22/-
COLONSAY	20/-	10/6	LOCHMADDY and LOCHEPORT, Direct Route	54/2	17/6
IONA, BUNESSAN	25/-	10/6	Do. do. via Harris	60/3	22/3
COLL, TIREE	31/6	12/6	SOAY, ELGOLL, Direct Route	40/-	15/-
CASTLEBAY, Direct Route	39/10	15/-	Do. do. via Harris	82/-	31/-
Do. via Harris	80/3	31/5	CARBOST, STRUAN, PORTNALONG, Direct Route	46/-	15/-
LOCHBOISDALE, Direct Route	45/9	15/-	Do. do. do. via Harris	80/3	27/6
Do. via Harris	74/3	28/1	DUNVEGAN, POOLTIEL, Direct Route	55/-	17/6
SKIPPORT, Direct Route	48/-	15/-	Do. do. via Harris	70/-	25/-
Do. via Harris	60/3	22/6	UIG, STEIN, Direct Route	55/-	17/6
CARNAN, Direct Route	49/-	15/-	Do. do. via Harris	70/-	25/-
Do. via Harris	60/3	22/3	HARRIS PORTS	60/-	20/-
KALLIN, Direct Route	50/-	15/-	* Sleeping Berth, 2/6 extra.		

NOTE.—On ST. KILDA, LOCH ROAG and ROUND SKYE CRUISES, Passengers to above ports whose journey embraces the Extended Cruises require to pay the extended fare in addition to the ordinary route fare.

CRUISE SAILING DATES AND FARES.

WESTERN ISLES	30th March, 3rd, 11th, 13th, 20th and 24th April, 1st, 4th and 11th May, 25th and 28th September.	* Board included £9.
ST. KILDA	25th May, 1st, 15th and 22nd June, 13th and 17th July, 3rd and 17th August.	
LOCH ROAG, LEWIS	5th June, 6th July, 7th August, and 7th September.	* Board included £10
LOCH SCAVAIG for LOCH CORUISK	15th May, 26th June, 27th July, 24th and 28th August, 14th and 18th September.	
ROUND THE ISLE OF SKYE	22nd May, 12th June, 3rd and 24th July, 14th August and 4th September.	

* Berths in Four-berthed Rooms 2/6 extra, in Two-berthed Rooms and Deck Cabins 5/- extra.

☞ All FREIGHTS must be PREPAID, except for PORTASKAIG, OBAN and TOBERMORY, and senders by Railway or Carrier must instruct the latter to pay through.

For further particulars, apply in Portaskaig to A. CURRIE & CO.; in Oban to DUNCAN MACDOUGALL, Railway Pier and Albany Street, Telephone, Oban 54 ; in Tobermory to JOHN M'FARLANE ; in Greenock to JAS. S. MILLAR, Customhouse Quay, Telephone, Greenock 686 ; or to—

McCALLUM, ORME & CO., LTD.,
45 UNION STREET, GLASGOW, C.1.

Telegraphic Address—" M'CALLUM, GLASGOW." Telephones—CENTRAL 7126/7/8.

.·. FOR CONDITIONS OF CARRIAGE SEE BACK HEREOF.

Liners of the Clyde

A nostalgic history of 24 ships built on the Clyde between 1910 and 1970. All the liners are illustrated by the well-known marine artist, John Nicholson, and most of the paintings were commissioned especially for this publication.

John Nicholson has also provided the excellent supporting text to accompany his colour illustrations.

A4 format. £8.95 plus 55p post and packing from the publishers.

Steamers of the Clyde

The magazine, Scottish Field, first published Steamers of the Clyde in 1967. It was a book containing a selection of histories of Clyde vessels, written by the late George Stromier and illustrated by marine artist John Nicholson. The book quickly became a collector's item and is long since 'out of print'.

The long awaited reprint was published in 1992. The original text was carefully examined and updated by Ian MacLagan and two motor ships which appeared in the original edition were omitted in favour of Duchess of Argyll, Saint Columba and Waverley resulting in a history of 24 vessels.

John Nicholson once again provided the illustrations. Many of his original drawings were replaced with more recent and even better artwork which allows the reader to savour the colours of the steamers, many of which were scrapped before colour photography became popular.

A4 format. £6.95 plus 55p post and packing from the publishers.

Memories of the Clyde

DUCHESS OF FIFE
1903 – 1953

Over 60 black and white photographs chart the building and 50 year working life of one of the Clyde's most famous Paddle Steamers. The centre spread features main deck and rigging plan and the cover illustration is by marine artist John Nicholson.

A4 format. £4.95 plus 55p post and packing from the publishers.

HART & WILL

2d Churchill Way, Bishopbriggs,
Glasgow G64 2RH. Telephone 0141-772 6911.